JUNGLE
Animals Can't Be Kind, Right?

Contributing Authors

Davenport Public School - Aylmer, Ontario

Miss Beth Buchanan's Grade 6 Class:

Grace Smith

Caden Lautebach

Ashley Bergen

Rhyan Hewbank

Ryder Stokley

Rachel Ross

Brooklyn Siwek

Noah Wiebe

Contributing Authors

Springfield Public School - Springfield, Ontario

Barb Esler's Grade 1/2 Class:

Emily Connor

Ethan Geerts

Troy Giesbrecht

Lilah Goodwill

Casey Huigenbos

Sydney Janzen

Justin Kloosterman

Jackson Lake

Mykah Lothi

Sophia Sawatzky

Kaidy Shackelton

James Stannard

Bentley Vantyghem

Korbin Walcarius

Connor Wall

Olivia Wilson

Contributing Authors

Springfield Public School - Springfield, Ontario

Tena Smithson's Grade 2/3 Class:

Anneka Drader	Abby Sawatzky
Daniel Epp	Ella Spence
Branden Hiebert	Taylor Telfer
Danielle Krahn	Dagon Thibodeau
Caden Lindsay	Liam Wall
Riley Lovell	Caleb Corless
Anika McAdam	Tyler Fehr
Addy Newell	Roman Schmitt
Annie Peters	Nolan Shackelton

Contributing Authors

West Nissouri Public School - Thorndale, Ontario

Jenn Griffin-Murrell's Grade 2/3 Class:

Jenna Gooder	Brooklynn Chilvers
Abigail Strubin	Kade Dobinson
Trestyn Veldman	Noah Pranger
Burke Latuszak	Taylor Sabino
Reese Angus	Sparrow Mund
Spencer Granville	Mack Smith
Abby Russell	Jaxon Wein
Caiden Mills	Charlie Pratt
Harlyn Tilson	Walker Waem
Reid Quinlan	Sylas Phan

Contributing Authors

South Dorchester Public School - Belmont, Ontario

Patti Wakem's Grade 3 Class:

Maija Berkelmans

Owen Charlton

Justin Cooper

Kayla De Angelis

Brayan Goetz

Benji Gould

Alex Harkness

Oliver Hill

Madison Knelsen

Ethan Johnson-Hoxar

Ruby Legg

Kaeden Leibold

Natalie Marques

Lucy Millard

Clintan Noble

Cody Rogers

Bella Stahlbaum

Cordela Tursa

Luke Willsie

Molly Wilson

ACKNOWLEDGMENTS

A very special thank you to all those who help make Write to Give happen. Each year, the program continues to grow and have a bigger impact on Canadian and international students. This would not happen, if it were not for the hard work of the teachers who have helped implement this program.

Thank you to our teachers, Beth Buchanan, Barb Esler, Tena Smithson, Jenn Griffin-Murrell and Patti Wakem.

Thank you to my team of editors, designers and family who have helped with W2G 2018.

Thank you,

Amy McLaren

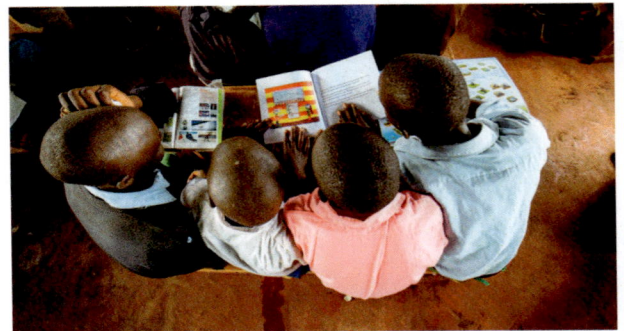

Jungle Animals Can't Be Kind, Right?

One hot, sunny day, Lion was resting in the long green grass near the river. He was there with his friend Elephant. They were resting in the shade of a big tree. Elephant was chewing grass and smacking her lips. Giraffe walked slowly out of the jungle to join the group. They were all hot and sweaty. Lion's stomach was growling because he had not eaten all day. Giraffe walked to the edge of the river and leaned down to take a drink of water. As he took a drink, he watched the fish swimming in the water.

All of a sudden there was a noise coming from the jungle.

"Hey everybody, did you hear that?" said Giraffe.

They all stopped to listen carefully. Lion dragged himself up and told the others to follow him. Together they quietly walked towards the sound. They were curious about the noise.

The noise grew extremely loud as they got closer. It was so loud the nocturnal animals could not sleep and the leaves were shaking on the trees. The lion king was not PLEASED because the animals in his jungle were not happy.

He roared, "WHAT'S THE PROBLEM!"

The chimps were quick to blame the group of cheetahs who were cheating at chess. The cheetahs were quick to blame the chattering chimps.

Lion shook his head so hard in frustration that his crown flew off his head. He thought that a chilly drink of water from the river might help him to cool down and think.

After his drink Lion felt he could help the cheetah and chimps solve their problem. BUT when he returned to the jungle he realized he had a problem of his own. His crown was missing.

Where could it have gone?

During all the commotion, the slithering snake caught a glimpse of something shiny. He snuck down from his tree to get a better look. Once he got down, he discovered it was the King's crown.

"Oh my! Its the royal crown. I must keep it safe!" he said to himself.

He carefully picked up the crown and put it around his neck. He slithered back up the tree and placed it on a thick leafy branch where it would be protected until King Lion came back.

Suddenly, while he was relaxing in his tree, Snake heard someone shouting for help. He looked down and saw King Lion.

He quickly slithered down the tree, bringing the crown with him.

Lion saw him and said "What are you doing with my crown?"

"I found it lying on the dirty jungle ground and I wanted to protect it your Majesty."

"Oh really? Thank you! I've been looking for this all day!" King Lion cried with glee.

Snake smiled with pride. "You're very welcome, your majesty."

"I shall throw a party at 7:00 tonight to celebrate my crown being returned, and everyone is invited!" Lion cried to the whole jungle.

Right away, preparations were put into place. The elephants made eggs. The cheetahs made cotton candy. The monkeys munched on mangoes. And the tigers put on their tuxedos!

Finally, it was time for the party. The King Lion stood on his podium in front of the crowd of rowdy animals and cheered: "Let's go party animals!"

The cheetahs set up a fair and honest chess game. The elephants marched in an organised way. The tigers got not a single speck of dirt on their tuxedos. And the king set out a giant steak for all animals to eat.

Snake smiled at King Lion. "I like this party."

"Me too."

WORLD TEACHER AID

World Teacher Aid is a Canadian charity committed to improving education throughout the developing world with a focus on IDP settlements (Internally Displaced Persons – communities that have been uprooted from their homes). Our current projects are within Kenya and Ghana.

As a charity we are committed to providing access to education for students within settled IDP Camps. We accomplish this vision through the renovation and/or construction of schools.

Before we begin working with a community, we ensure that they are on board with the goal. A community must be settled and show leadership before we commit to a project. We also look for commitment from the Government, ensuring that if we step in and build the school, that they will help support the ongoing expenses, such as teachers salaries, and more.

World Teacher Aid

AUTOGRAPHS

AUTOGRAPHS

Made in the USA
Lexington, KY
11 April 2018